JOHN BANNER

HIS LIFE AND TIMES

BY

MICK MANISE

Grosvenor House
Publishing Limited

This book is published by
Grosvenor House Publishing Ltd
28-30 High Street, Guildford, Surrey, GU1 3EL.
www.grosvenorhousepublishing.co.uk

A CIP record for this book
is available from the British Library

ISBN 978-1-78623-758-3

CONTENTS

By the Same Author

Captain Desmond Ellis Hubble;
from cradle to grave

For further information, please go to;
mickmanisebooks.uk

ACKNOWLEDGEMENTS

I am very grateful to my wife Christine for support and ideas, Mrs Janet Lowe for answering my endless enquiries about the Banner family. Suzanne Oatley for proof reading.

The following have been inexhaustible sources for information:
Imperial War Museum
Commonwealth War Graves Commission
The Long, Long trail web site
The Wardrobe (Wiltshire regiment museum).
National Archives
Worcester Library and History Centre
Worcestershire County Council Record Office
A Carpenter's Tale
O.S. Maps
British History online
The 1st Battalion of the Wiltshire Regiment in the Great War. Edwin Astill

I am particularly grateful to The Trustees of the Rifles Wardrobe and Museum Trust for their kind permission to reproduce extracts of the War Diary of the 1st Battalion of the Wiltshire Regiment and assistance in its interpretation. The diary has been an invaluable tool to determine John Banner's story and in places I have quoted the diary in the format in which it appears in the book as I believe the first interpretation to be important and any further changes have the danger of creating a Chinese Whispers scenario. All quotes are in italics.

Where the internet has been used, information has not been used until verified from a separate source.

DEDICATION

There are many forms of bravery and I am proud to say that I have two sons who have, in their own way, displayed two different types. I dedicate this book to them, Paul and Tom Manise.

In Memory of
Private JOHN BANNER

19626, 1st Battalion, Wiltshire Regiment
Killed In Action on 6th July 1916

Remembered with honour
THIEPVAL MEMORIAL

Commemorated in perpetuity by
the Commonwealth War Graves Commission

INTRODUCTION

Whilst on a motorcycling holiday some years ago, I was asked to stop by Thiepval near to Albert in the Somme district of France to collect a photograph of the memorial there and the inscription for a John Banner.

John had all but been forgotten and but for a distant family member compiling a family tree, would soon have been forgotten to history. John's military record had survived the bombing of World War Two and with other sources provided sufficient detail for his brief story to be told.

I hope that this book keeps John's memory alive and is a fitting tribute to his sacrifice.

FOREWORD

John Banner was my Uncle on my maternal side, whilst I had other uncles, I grew up knowing that John had been killed in the awful carnage of the First World War and that this had left an inerasable sadness on my family.

John was killed at the age of 20, he never knew the long and lasting love of a wife, the adoration that children have of their father, nor any of the other wonderful things that a long and fruitful life brings. His sacrifice and that of thousands of other young men of his generation was supposed to be the last to end all wars, but it did not, it would be a tragic waste if his name was not honoured and remembered.

Gwen Hill
Sutton Coldfield
2016

PART I

THE BANNER FAMILY

ANSLEM BANNER

John Banner's story starts with his parents. His father, Anslem Banner, was born 10.10.1859 (died 26.1.1914.) in Little Heath, near Bromsgrove, Worcestershire. He was one of five children.

In 1881, the census shows his family as resident at Watery Lane in the hamlet of Long Eye, The Lickey, Bromsgrove. At this point Anslem has left home and is living at Townsend Mill, Birmingham Road, Bromsgrove where he was employed as a servant Corn Miller. Anslem's family were all employed as nail makers.

There is no record of education for Anslem and there is a possibility that he may never have attended school as compulsory education to the minimum age of 11 years was introduced in 1893 when he was 34 years old. To get a general feel for this, in 1881 Anslem Banner was 21 years old, his parents and three of his siblings are all employed as nail makers, the youngest being 11. The youngest sibling, a sister, was three years old and a status is not declared. In the next house a boy of five is shown as a scholar and in the next house a girl of four also is a scholar, all other occupants are nail makers. At the same time, a little further up the road, the children of Edward Marsh, a builder employing two people, living at Little Heath Farm, were aged seven, nine, 13 and 15 years old and are all described as scholars. Certainly if Anslem Banner did receive any education it will have been over by the time he was 11 years old and he was then either employed in the cottage industry of nail making or taken in at the Mill to train as a miller.

Anslem married Emily Joice in 1889 at Baptist Chapel, Denton in the District of Hardingstone, Northampton. His address at the time was Spring Road, Northampton and his bride's is recorded as Denton. Their home is near to the river Nene and in its valley. Ordinance Survey maps (OS) of the day show a number of corn mills in the area where Anslem would have been employed. Emily died on 20th June 1890 of;

"Paralysis 7 days (one month after childbirth)".

There is no record of a birth so we can assume the baby was still-born, there being no requirement at the time to register this event. Anslem stayed in the area for a short while as on the 1891 census he was living in Fetter Street, Northampton and is listed as a widower, occupation Journeyman Miller, living with him was his younger brother, Samuel, whose occupation was Miller's Labourer.

Anslem's trail at this time is one of moving about which does coincide with the history of the water corn mills in the latter half of the 19th century. Corn was being imported in quantity and docks were installing steam powered mills to refine the corn direct from the ships. This inevitably led to a decline in the small water mill industry and Anslem was no doubt forced to move about to find the work of which he by now enjoyed the status of Journeyman.

Between April 1891 and February 1892 Anslem met and married Emily Butler.

THE NAIL MAKING INDUSTRY AND BROMSGROVE AREA

Anslem Banner's family were all nail makers and this seems to have been how most members of the family in his past and contemporaneous history had been employed. Nail making was a popular occupation in the Bromsgrove area and Anslem seems to have shunned tradition by pursuing a career as a miller. The industry was largely fuelled by family run cottage concerns and although there were nail making factories in existence with machines making nails, the technology had not totally eliminated the need for handmade wrought iron nails. The industry gives an understanding of the world Anslem and therefore John Banner were born and lived in.

A wonderful picture of life in the Bromsgrove area is given in the book 'A Carpenter's Tale' written from the notes left behind by Arthur James (1878-1963) which were found after his death by his son.

Nail making in the Bromsgrove area was a cottage industry in decline from 1860 onwards due to factories set up in the cities, such as Birmingham, during the Industrial Revolution. Whole families were employed and conducted the business from a nail shop at the rear of their houses. The nail shop contained a furnace for heating irons. The nails were made from wrought iron and forged by hand by hammering a heated iron rod to a point, cutting it to the required length and then wedging it in an iron hole and pounding a head onto it.

The nail making families lived in great poverty and relied on all sorts of side lines to make ends meet. Most families kept chickens and ducks which roosted at night in lofts above the nail shop. Due to the poverty children were not forced to go to school as their labour was needed in the family businesses. In 1888, when Arthur James was 10 years old, schools charged a weekly fee payable on Mondays. However, during strikes by the nail makers the fees were usually waived. Some children on reaching standard four were allowed to attend school on half days, one week in the mornings the next in the afternoon. Head masters had to insist on seeing birth certificates to verify school leaving ages as children would try to leave early to create income for the family.

On Birmingham Road Norton, near to where the Arthur James lived, was a Union Workhouse. This institution housed the jobless, sick, aged and mentally ill. By 1890 this house served 20 local authorities and housed 300 men women and children. The 1881 census shows a number of persons named Banner resident in the workhouse, of which one was William Banner, John's great grandfather. He must have become destitute, his wife had died young in 1841 and he seems to have drifted around after that lodging with various people. In 1871 he was lodging with an Ann Banner, so sometime between 1871 and 1881 he ended up in the workhouse. His occupation is listed as nail maker and he was 70 years of age in 1881, he died in 1891.

Sanitation for families in the area was very basic. Baths were owned by very few people and washing was conducted in a sink. Water was drawn from a number of shallow wells and the highly contaminated Spadesbourne brook. (This was the water power for Townsend Mill where Anslem lived and worked at the time of the 1881 census.) Clean water was first piped into Bromsgrove by the recently formed East Worcestershire Waterworks Company in 1882, but in the early years few people took advantage of it. Running water was viewed as a luxury rather than a necessity. Toilet facilities were generally an open midden, (a dump for domestic waste), adjacent to the pantry and near to a water pump. Sewerage was dug out by the 'Night Soil Men' who commenced work after midnight. The sound of them coming near to your house was a signal to shut the windows as the smell was appalling. This practise of sewerage disposal was still in use in some places into the early 1930s. This sanitation, or lack of it, was the cause of the Typhoid epidemic of 1887, hardly a house in Norton was spared a casualty if not a death. This epidemic coincided with the first official recording of a drought and sewerage was draining into a lowering water table which people were drinking.

Superficially it sounds all doom and gloom but there are also lovely stories recounted of boys placing turfs over nail house chimneys and then running away before the choking nailers caught them, or driving a newly acquired cockerel into the domain of established cocks and revelling at the ensuing fight. It was a place and era of wonderful characters such as Tommy Kia who was in the habit of visiting the James's home on a Sunday morning, at breakfast time, after a night in the pub. This was to the annoyance of Arthur's mother but Tommy always brought a cigar (which were handed out free in the pub). Tommy did not smoke so saved it for James's father in exchange for a cup of tea with accompanying pick me up.

Living nearby was Miss Hornblower who is described as '*a dwarf of an old lady*', very clever at making potions and ointments'. Her house was like a doctor's surgery and people came from far and wide with ailments. My favourite character is Blind Jack. Jack Wakeman had not been born blind but having become so he made his living in various ways. He delivered newspapers with the assistance of a friend's young son. He sold nuts in the pubs and carried dice with him for the drinkers to hold a raffle, winner take all, Jack taking his cut. He was a very strong man and was called upon to deal with trouble makers in the pubs and woe betide anyone caught in his grip. He knew all his pigeons by touch and loved football, being taken to the matches by friends and given a running commentary. These commentaries must have been very accurate as he always took part in the post-match discussions in the pub. The Hop Pole pub on Birmingham Road, Bromsgrove was a favourite watering hole where he had a favourite seat which was vacated for him whenever he entered. A brass plaque was placed on this seat and sold on with the pub as a fixture and fitting. The original pub has been knocked down and rebuilt but the plaque to Blind Jack is still there on the first bench on the right upon entering.

This was the Bromsgrove the Banner family lived in. Social conditions varying from the total poverty of those in the work-house to substantial middle class dwellings which occur all in the same area. One method of dealing with the poor was to give assisted passage to the colonies. Between 1880 and 1914, the peak period for this practice, 13 million people left the UK for Canada, Australia, New Zealand and South Africa. The most popular destination was the ex-colony of America. Even though the traditional industries were declining due to industrialisation the Banner family stuck it out and remained in the area.

EMILY BANNER

John's mother, Emily Butler (1862 – 3.11.1902) was born in Aston, Birmingham. Her father was a shoe and boot maker with his own shop. According to the 1861 census he had a shop in Lichfield Road, Aston but by the 1871 census he had moved his shop to Sutton Road, Erdington, Birmingham. In 1901 his shop was at 18 High Street, Erdington (this building was still there in 2009 and used as a florist's shop). In 1881 Emily Butler was living with the Collier family (also on Sutton Road, Erdington) and employed as a general servant. Mr Collier was a Florist/Grocer. In 1891 Emily was still living in Sutton Road, Erdington and was still employed as a general servant, but for a William Wright who was a Nurseryman/Florist.

Emily Butler married Anslem Banner on 1st February 1892 at Erdington Parish Church. There is no clue as to how they met, at this time Anslem was resident in Lawford, Rugby and she was still living in Erdington so at this stage it is a mystery. It may appear unseemly for John's parents to wed so soon after the death of Anslem's first wife, but in the 19th century marriage was a very popular institution. The benefits for men were household labour, sex and children; the benefits for women were support and a limited legal standing. Between 1852 and 1870 Mary Ann Cotton married and murdered four husbands. Between these dates she also found time to murder one lover and 15 of her own children. The case gives an insight into the necessity and desirability of marriage for both men and women.

It would appear that Anslem and Emily lived in Rugby after the wedding as that is where their first child Ernest James was born.

Emily died on 3rd November 1902. The address on the death certificate is just given as Little Heath. The cause of death was

"Phthisis and Consumption 6 months", now better known as Tuberculosis or T.B.

JOHN BANNER AND SIBLINGS

Anslem and Emily had five children of which John was the third.

1. Ernest James Banner (1893 – 1983) born in Rugby, Warwickshire.
2. Anslem Frederick Banner (23.10.1894 – 19.4.1966) Born in Burcot, Worcestershire.
3. John.
4. Frank Banner (1898 – 1957) Born in Lickey End, Worcestershire.
5. Martha Banner (17.2.1900 – 22.2.1959) Born in Little Heath, Worcestershire.

Martha Banner, Ernest James Banner and Frank Banner & family

John Banner was born on 20th December 1895, in Burcot, Worcestershire. At this stage his father is still described as a miller, but we know that by this date his status was that of Journeyman corn miller. Again there is no evidence of what John received by means of an education but by this time the minimum school leaving age was 12, it having been raised from 11 in 1899.

In 1901 John was five years old and the family was living at No.1 Little Heath, The Lickey, North Bromsgrove. This is described on the census as '*a block of 3 cottage premises*'. John's elder brother, Anslem Frederick Banner, was also born in Burcot. John's two younger siblings were born in Lickey End and Little Heath respectively, I suspect that these last two addresses are one and the same and the full address would be Little Heath, Lickey End. Of the five children the census shows three different places of birth so it is likely that the family moved around due to Anslem Banner's work commitments and that the family moved from Rugby to an unknown address in Burcot and from there to Little Heath. Apart from the first child being born in Rugby all the others were born in villages of Bromsgrove which have now been incorporated within the town.

On 3rd November 1902 John's mother Emily died of TB.

The 1911 census shows the family still resident at Little Heath minus Ernest James Banner who by now was 17 years old. Anslem Banner is described as head of the household, a widower and a gardener by profession in employment. There is a requirement on this census to number the rooms in the house. The kitchen was counted as a room but excluded the scullery, landing, closet, lobby or bathroom; the rooms totalled three for father, three sons and a daughter Martha who is described as 11 years old and at school. It is interesting to note that John's elder brother Anslem Frederick Banner was 16 years old and working as a Joiners apprentice. Both John who was 15 and Frank 13 are working as farm labourers. With Martha at school at 11 and Frank working at 13, this gives us an accurate assumption that John's schooldays ended when he was 12 years old.

The census also shows living at Little Heath Farm, William Tilt with his wife three daughters and son. It is not known whether William Tilt the farmer was related to the Tilt brothers of Birmingham Road, but it does seem coincidental that in 1911 one son is employed as a joiner's apprentice and two sons are farm labourers then by 1914 the family are at Uplands Road and John is now working at Tilt brothers.

On 21st January 1914 Anslem Banner died aged 54. The cause of death is recorded as *(1) Influenza and (2) Acute Bronchitis heart failure*. The death was reported by his eldest son Ernest

James Banner and the address is recorded as Uplands Road Norton Bromsgrove. This address coincides with the army records for John's enlistment. This road still exists and is shown as in the close proximity of the site of Townsend Mill, the death certificate records Anslem's profession as Journeyman Corn Miller. There is no way of telling when the family moved to Uplands Road from Little Heath nor whether Anslem worked at the Mill, but we do know that John was employed at Tilts Brothers at this time and the address is advantageous for work at both the Mill and Tilts yard on Birmingham Road. Kelly's directory for 1912 shows this company as a *'Builders and sanitary engineers'*.

Tilt Bros. was a company originally formed by Joseph Tilt in partnership with a carpenter named William Weaver; Joseph Tilt was responsible for the brick work. Tilt and Weaver separated and Joseph Tilt ran his business from the Hop Pole Pub which he also owned and ran. In 1906 the company was handed over to Joseph's sons and re-named Tilt Bros. with premises on Birmingham Road, Bromsgrove near to the Hop Pole. It is not known in what capacity John Banner was employed at Tilts but the company was involved in major construction for the county and employed builders and carpenters. It is likely that John was serving an apprenticeship in one of the building trades. Looking at the time scale there is no doubt that he was known to Arthur James (A Carpenter's Tale) and the County Architect, Alfred Vernon Rowe.

PART II

WORLD WAR ONE

O n 28th June 1914 the Archduke Franz Ferdinand of Austria, heir to the Austro-Hungarian throne, was assassinated by a Serbian nationalist, Gavrilo Princip. Austria-Hungary's resulting demands against the Kingdom of Serbia led to the activation of a series of alliances which within weeks saw all of the major European powers at war. As a consequence of the global empires of many European nations, the war soon spread worldwide. Germany invaded neutral Belgium and refused to withdraw its troops, as a consequence Britain declared war on Germany On 3rdAugust 1914 and the British Expeditionary Force was sent to France. Britain also declared war on Austria on 12th August.

On 28th November 1914 John enlisted in the British army at Birmingham recruitment office. He was without doubt a volunteer and answering the call of his country to arms as conscription was not introduced until 1916.

WARTIME VOLUNTARY RECRUITMENT PRIOR TO CONSCRIPTION

Recruitment Poster

On his appointment as Secretary of State for War, shortly after Britain's declaration of war, Field-Marshal Lord Kitchener issued a call for volunteers to increase the size of the army. He did not believe that the Territorial Force, which at the time was 11 divisions strong, was an appropriate structure for doing this. The men would only have to enlist '*for the duration of the war*' but legally they were joining the regular army. The volunteers were generally assigned to units of the New Armies, although many once trained were posted to replace losses in the existing regular army units.

The wartime volunteers had a choice of the branch of service and the regiment they joined. They had to meet the same physical criteria as the regulars, but men who had previously served in the army would now be accepted up to the age of 45. There are many recorded instances of under age and indeed overage men being accepted into the service. It was not necessary to produce evidence of age or even of one's name in order to enlist. Kitchener had hoped for 100,000 volunteers in the first six months and a maximum of 500,000 altogether as this was the maximum that the existing factories were capable of equipping. The public response to Kitchener's appeal was rapid and in the first month 500,000 volunteers came forward, this soon died down to an average of 100,000 men per month for the next 18 months.

While no doubt many were inspired to enlist by the news, drum-beating and pressure to conform, some modern historians have argued that men joined up for all manner of reasons, including a natural desire to quit a humdrum or arduous job, take a chance of seeing another country or to escape family or other troubles. Volunteers usually had a considerable choice about which branch of the service they joined. Many travelled considerable distances to attend a depot or recruiting office for a particular unit. They would be attracted to a particular regiment or corps by its reputation, or the fact that it was the local one or where they had relatives or pals. The Pals system was introduced as a means of enlisting manpower in quantity. Workmates were allowed to enlist and choose a regiment with the promise that they would then serve together.

There is evidence within the Banner family and from the diary notes of Arthur James, (A Carpenter's Tale), that John Banner chose to join the army at an enlistment station away from home and also to join a non-local regiment. John's brothers Frank and Anslem served during the war in the Worcester Regiment and the Worcester Territorials. Arthur James recalls, post war, that the Worcester County Architect, Alfred Vernon Rowe, visited work sites for Tilt Brothers and during lunch breaks he and the Tilt men who had served under him during the war would '*talk of their doings in France*'. It does not describe numbers but the fact that he gives this description would indicate that the chosen regiment locally was the Worcester regiment of which Vernon Rowe returned from war in 1919 a Major and continued to serve with the Worcester territorials concluding his service as a Brevet-Colonel.

After the form filling and the examinations, called attestation, the process concluded by the recruit taking the King's Shilling and the recruiting Sergeant taking his sixpence per man. The recruit then went home, receiving his joining instructions and travel warrant a day or two later in the post.

ENLISTMENT

John was initially posted to the Oxford and Buckinghamshire Light Infantry, regimental number 16566.

John was issued with a uniform, a pay and record book and identity tags.

Pay book and fibre identity tags

The chances of finding the record of a First World War soldier are not good as 75 percent were stored in London and destroyed in the Blitz of World War Two. We can assume, however, from the regimental records that John was posted to the 3rd (Reserve) Battalion. At the outbreak of war the regiment consisted of three battalions. The 1st Battalion was stationed in Ahmednagar, India, attached to 17th Indian Brigade of 6th (Poona) Division, Indian Army. On 27th November 1914 it was moved to Mesopotamia where they fought the Turks. Here they suffered very heavy casualties, were besieged at Kut-el-Amara and eventually starved into surrender. Of the 300 men who were taken prisoner only 90 survived the war. The 2nd Battalion was stationed in Aldershot, part of 5th Brigade in 2nd Division. On 14th August 1914 they landed at Boulogne. In 1914 they achieved fame at Nonne Boschen by routing the Prussian Potsdam Guards. The 3rd (reserve) Battalion was stationed in Oxford, a depot/training unit, it moved to Portsmouth in August 1914 and went on to Dover in October 1917.This battalion would have been where John was first stationed to receive his basic training. John and his fellow volunteers would have found themselves housed under canvas, training in civilian clothes and using walking sticks for rifle drill until the factories were expanded to deal with the increased demand for equipment.

BASIC TRAINING

The principles and details of training were laid down in the Field Service Regulations and in Army Publications such as "Infantry Training 1914". Basic training for ordinary Tommies lasted for between three – six months and began with physical fitness, close order drill, march discipline, essential field craft, and musketry. Later, as the soldier specialised (in the infantry, for example, as a rifleman, machine gunner, rifle grenadier, signaller or bomber) he would receive courses of instruction relevant to his role. In particular, as he was approaching being warned for the active fronts, he would receive basic training in first aid, gas defence, wiring and other aspects. This training continued when he was on active service. Basic training taught a man individual and unit discipline, how to follow commands, how to march, some basic field skills and how to safely handle his weapons. Many men, especially the volunteers, believed there was too much '*Bull*', designed to suppress the individual spirit, ingenuity and initiative out of a man. Many men arrived at the fighting fronts utterly unprepared for the experience as warfare had changed and become trench bound. Trench training commenced when the soldier arrived in France.

THE OXFORDSHIRE AND BUCKINGHAMSHIRE LIGHT INFANTRY (43RD AND 52ND FOOT)

Ox & Bucks Badge

The 43rd and 52nd Regiments were independent of each other until the Cardwell reorganisation of the Army in 1881 recognised the historical links between the 43rd and 52nd and decreed that they should become the 1st and 2nd Battalions of The Oxfordshire Light Infantry, though the old regimental numbers continued in unofficial use. The combined regiment was based at a new Depot at Cowley, Oxford. In 1908 'Buckinghamshire' was added to the title. During World War One the regiment won 59 battle honours, two Victoria Crosses and lost 5880 dead. In 1966 the Regiment was amalgamated with the 2nd Green Jacket (The Kings Royal Rifle Corps) and the 3rd Green Jackets (The Rifle Brigade) to form The Royal Green Jackets.

CONSTRUCTION OF AN INFANTRY BATTALION

The battalion was the basic tactical unit of the infantry of the British army in the Great War of 1914-1918. At full establishment

15

it consisted of a Battalion headquarters, four Companies and 1,007 men, of whom 30 were officers.

BATTALION HQ

The battalion was usually commanded by an officer with the rank of Lieutenant-Colonel with a Major as Second-in-Command. Battalion HQ also had three other officers; a Captain or Lieutenant filled the role of Adjutant, a Captain or Lieutenant as the Quartermaster and an officer of the Royal Army Medical Corps attached as Medical Officer. Battalion HQ also included the Regimental Sergeant-Major plus a number of specialist roles filled by Sergeants; Quartermaster, Drummer, Cook, Pioneer, Shoemaker, Transport, Signaller, Armourer and Orderly Room Clerk.

A Corporal and four Privates of the Royal Army Medical Corps were attached to Battalion HQ for water duties; a Corporal and 15 Privates were employed as Signallers; 10 Privates were employed as Pioneers (on construction, repair and general engineering duties); 11 Privates acted as Drivers for the horse-drawn transport; 16 acted as stretcher-bearers (these often being the musicians of the Battalion Band); six Privates acted as officers batmen (personal servants) and two as orderlies for the Medical Officer.

COMPANIES

The four Companies, usually lettered A to D, numbered 227 personnel at full establishment. Each was commanded by a Major or Captain, with a Captain as Second-in-Command. Company HQ included a Company Sergeant-Major, a Company Quartermaster Sergeant, two Privates acting as batmen and three as drivers. The body of the company was divided into four Platoons, each of which was commanded by a subaltern. In total, the four Platoons consisted of eight Sergeants, 10 Corporals, four Drummers, four Batmen and 188 Privates. Each Platoon was subdivided into four Sections, each of 12 men under the command of an NCO (Non-Commissioned Officer).

ALSO ON THE STRENGTH OF THE BATTALION

Each battalion had, in 1914, a Machine Gun Section consisting of a Lieutenant, a Sergeant, a Corporal, two Drivers, a Batman and 12 Privates trained in the maintenance, transport, loading and firing of the Vickers heavy machine gun. These men made up two six-man gun teams. By February 1915 the allocation of machine-guns to each battalion had been doubled to four. In February 1916 the gunners were formally transferred from their regiments into the newly-formed Machine Gun Corps. To replace the loss of these guns the infantry battalions received four Lewis light machine guns. By the opening of the 1916 Somme offensive this had been increased to 16 guns per battalion, and early in 1918 this was increased again to 36 guns. The fire-power of the battalion was thus considerably increased throughout the war.

BATTALION EQUIPMENT

Battalion Transport consisted of 13 riding and 43 draught and pack horses. They provided the power for drawing the six ammunition carts, two water carts, three General Service Wagons (for tools and machine guns) and the Medical Officer's Maltese Cart. The Signallers had use of nine bicycles.

Most men carried a rifle, which for the regular battalions was the short magazine Lee-Enfield. The only exceptions were officers, pipers, drummers, buglers and the five men in each battalion who carried range-finding instruments. All those carrying a rifle, except the RSM and other Staff-Sergeants, were also armed with the sword-bayonet.

Other battalion equipment, over and above that carried by the men, included 120 shovels, 73 pickaxes, 20 felling axes, eight hand axes, 46 billhooks, 20 reaping hooks, a hand saw, 32 folding saws and eight crowbars. There was also a plethora of minor stores and spares.

The battalion also carried a certain quantity of ammunition, although this was backed up by the echelons of lines of communication and transport at brigade and divisional and levels. When added together, the ammunition supply per rifle came to 550 rounds per man. The battalion transport carried 32 boxes of 1,000 rounds, and each man could carry up to 120 rounds. The machine guns were each supplied with a total of 41,500 rounds of which 3,500 was carried with the gun, and 8,000 in regimental reserve.

THE WILTSHIRE REGIMENT

On 29th April 1915 John was transferred to the Wiltshire Regiment. This date is four months from his joining date and indicates that his stay with the Ox and Bucks was for basic training only.

Wiltshire Regiment Cap Badge

HISTORY

In January 1758 four companies of the 2nd/4th Regiment embarked from Plymouth, as Marines under the command of Major T Hardy, in five ships of Admiral Boscawin's fleet. The fleet sailed for Halifax, Nova Scotia, the mounting base for a seaborne attack on French Canada. Whilst these companies were on passage, the Royal Horse Guards (the name of the headquarters of the British

Army, not to be confused with the Cavalry Regiment of that name), decreed that the new second battalions throughout the army would be numbered as separate Regiments. Under this re-organisation the 2nd/4th Regiment became the 62nd Regiment of Foot.

Throughout the campaign the 62nd continued to serve as Marines, providing landing parties, manning ships and boats, transferring artillery pieces ashore and providing local protection for them.

The 62nd had won their first battle honours at Louisburg, but it was not awarded until 150 years later. To commemorate their service as Marines the 62nd were permitted to play 'Rule Britannia' after the Regimental March.

Early in 1782, the Commander in Chief laid down that County titles be given to Regiments of the Line, to encourage recruiting, the 62nd took the name of Wiltshire and henceforth became known as the 62nd (Wiltshire) Regiment.

The 1st Battalion of the Wiltshire regiment was given orders to mobilize at 5.45 p.m. on Tuesday 4th August 1914. Earlier that day Germany had invaded Belgium and on the previous day they had declared war on France. Britain's ultimatum to Germany expired at 11p.m. the same day. In just four days the battalion was able to report to brigade that mobilisation was complete. The next four days were spent on the ranges with musketry practise, route marches, medicals and administration such as the settling of accounts. Early on the morning of 13th August 1914 the battalion entrained for Southampton where they boarded ships bound for France.

The 1st Wiltshire War Diary records the following:

1st Wiltshire   Thursday 13th August 1914   England, Tidworth

7.22a.m. 1st Train Lieut Col A W Hasted Commanding.
Strength 505 all ranks.
2nd Train Major A S Barnes Commanding.
Strength 509 all ranks.
Left TIDWORTH

9.12 am. 1st Train arrived SOUTHAMPTON Docks and detrained at Shed 23.

11a.m. 1st Train commenced embarking on SS South Western: much delay in embarkation of vehicles as hatch very small and all shafts and the wheels of G.S. wagons had to be removed. All horses (these had to be boxed and slung) and vehicles on board by 4.15p.m.

4.15p.m. Troops embarked.

4.30p.m. Vessel sailed.

7.15p.m. Anchored in Sandown Bay.

10.45a.m. 2nd Train arrived at SOUTHAMPTON and commenced embarkation on S.S. Princess Ena.

2.30p.m. Cast off.

1st Wiltshire   **Friday 14th August 1914**   **France, [Rouen]**

5a.m. Got under way.

7.30a.m. 2nd party arrived at ROUEN and marched to camp at Mont St. Aignan.

8.45p.m. 1st party arrives at ROUEN. Disembarked and marched to camp at Mont St. Aignan.

Appx

The following officers landed with the Battn in France:-

Lieut Colonel A W Hasted, Commanding Officer; Major A S Barnes; Major P Roche; Capt F W Stoddart; Capt M C Richards; Capt W R A Dawes; Capt H R H Davies; Lieut J H M Mee; Lieut P S L Beaver;

Lieut W C Loder-Symonds; Lieut R H Broome; Lieut O G Browne; Lieut B H Goodhart; Lieut T H Wand-Tetley; Lieut K J P Oliphant; Lieut N D Stewart; Lieut E H B Richardson; 2nd Lieut F S Carrington;

2nd Lieut C C Morse; 2nd Lieut H W C Lloyd; 2nd Lieut E O Cruickshank; 2nd Lieut H W Roseveare; Capt & Adjutant P S Rowan;

Capt & Q M, W I Cordon; Lieut P S Power, R A M C, Medical Officer

"By their Deeds shall thee know them".

The great adventure had started with a general expectation that it would all be over by Christmas and everyone would then be back home to enjoy normal life. By 24th October the 1st Battalions strength had been reduced to 250 men, on the 4th November it was noted that the battalion had lost 26 officers and 1000 men, the equivalent of a whole battalion. By the end of the First World War the Wiltshire's had raised 11 Battalions which served in France, Flanders, Salonica, Gallipoli, Mesopotamia, India, Egypt and Ireland. It had also earned 60 battle honours. Captain Reginald Hayward of the Wiltshire's was awarded the Victoria Cross. The Wiltshire's death toll was heavy losing nearly 5,000 men dead or the equivalent of five of the battalions which served.

PART III

TO FRANCE AND BELGIUM

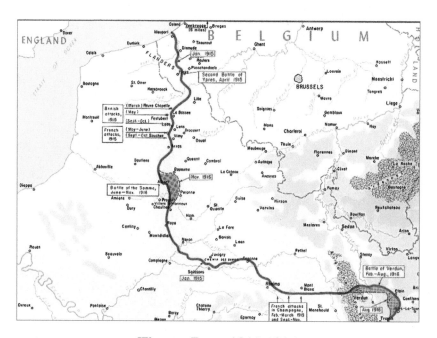

Western Front 1915-1916

John's Wiltshire Regimental number was 19626 and he was initially posted to 3rd Battalion in Exeter. This battalion was responsible for recruit training and posting soldiers to the front. John was then posted to 1st Battalion and embarked to

France on 4th May 1915. The period between joining the Regiment on 29th April and 4th May was presumably spent in pre deployment training.

Who can imagine the thoughts travelling through John's mind at this stage? His journey to France took five days; he was 18 years old and had no experience of the world outside of his home in Bromsgrove. He was a volunteer embarking on a great adventure to save the world from evil, what young man indoctrinated with the limited education given to those of the home front, about the conditions and dangers of life in the trenches would not be excited? His journey would have been completed by means of train, boat and converted London bus.

Bus convoy transporting troops in France

He joined the battalion on 9th May and his first day is best described by the battalion's war diary:

1st Wiltshire   Sunday 9th May 1915.   Belgium, Elzenwalle

Fairly quiet day. German aeroplane brought down by British just SE of ST ELOI.
One man killed. 2 men wounded.

The stress, danger and poor conditions for men in the trenches were a great drain on individual and unit moral. Incidents such as the downing of an enemy plane and the successful activities of snipers were used to great effect to boost morale. This must have been a good day to arrive and meet his new comrades as this incident would have been the main topic of conversation and 'one up for our side'!

Elsewhere on the 9th May the second battle of Artois commenced. This battle was from 9th May 1918 to June 1915 and was the most important part of the Allied spring offensive of 1915. It was hoped to capture Vimy Ridge, break through the German lines and advance into the Douai plain. This would cut key German railway lines and perhaps force them to retreat from their great salient bulging out into France. The French offensive would be launched by the Tenth Army, under General d'Urbal. It was supported by 1,200 guns with 200,000 shells, a huge amount for ammunition for 1915. The artillery bombardment began six days before the attack was due to go in.

The British attack at Aubers Ridge was a total failure. It cost the BEF 10,000 casualties and achieved nothing. In contrast, the French attack on 9th May opened with a dramatic success. Pétain's XXXIII corps advanced two and a half miles in the first hour and a half of the battle, and the 77th and Moroccan Divisions actually reached the crest of Vimy Ridge.

When John arrived on 9th May 1915 the battalion had been at rest at Dickebusche and had taken over P sector of the trenches at Elzenwalle on Sunday 2nd May, on this day three men had been injured, a further nine men had been injured and three killed by the time of John's arrival.

On 11th May the battalion was relieved at 9 p.m. and moved back for rest to Dickebusch. On this day one man was killed and one injured, presumably during the changeover of positions as on these occasions the communications trenches were targeted by enemy artillery and mortar fire because these trenches were full of men. The other notable event was the arrival of a new Battalion Commander, Major Blake. Lieutenant Colonel Halsted the previous Commander was one of the few original officers left and was relieved due to ill health.

Whilst at rest the Battalion would have completed fatigues and further training and on 15th May they were shelled between 5 and 6 p.m. with one man being wounded. Clearly a rest area was still not a safe place to be. Between 17th May and 21st May they moved back to take their positions again in P sector at Elzenwalle. During this time the sector was quiet but three men were wounded and two killed by enemy snipers.

This backwards and forwards routine continued until 3rd June when they were relieved and marched in the afternoon to Vlamertinghe where they went into huts. This must have been a luxury but on 4th June they were sent to visit Hooge defences in the evening and during the night took over from the Lincolns, the trenches were described as being in a very bad state and one man was wounded. The following day was spent improving the trenches.

The events of the 6th of June give a good picture of the daily dangers faced by John and his comrades. At 10 a.m. the enemy commenced a bombardment of the trenches occupied by the Wiltshires with a heavy and a medium Minenwerfer, (mine launcher, a type of mortar weapon). The mortars were finally silenced by British artillery at 11.30 a.m. and in that time it is recorded that 21 shots were fired resulting in two men killed and 20 wounded, a heavy toll for such a short time.

PART IV

LIFE IN THE TRENCHES

By the time John arrived in May 1915, conditions in the trenches had been improved a little compared to the first winter. Notes from the war diary are helpful in providing a picture of life for these men. Trench warfare was a relatively new concept, experience and a good flow of materials went a long way. The weather was a huge factor, in winter the removal of excess water was a greater problem than during summer. Also the location and geology of the area was important. Some trenches had to be made almost entirely from sand bags due to rocky ground and a high water table would also limit the depth of a trench. Hand pumps were employed to keep water out of the trenches but this must have been a continual battle during wet weather.

The below sketch of a trench system gives an idea of the problems involved.

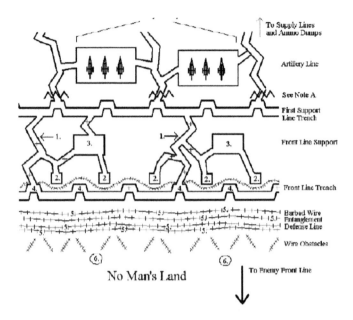

1 = Communications trench.
The communication trenches were used to move between the front and rear trenches. They were also used to transport injured men to the field hospitals.

2 = Machine gun positions.
The machine gun nest was where the machine guns were located. They were manned by two or three soldiers who fired on any advancing enemy.

3 = Bunkers.
The underground bunkers were used to store food, weapons and artillery. They were also used as command centres and had a telephone link to report information and receive instructions. The underground bunkers also offered the men protection from fire and the elements.

4 = Frontline trench.
Trenches were not built in straight lines. This was so that if the enemy managed to get into the front line trench they

would not have a straight firing line along the trench. Trenches were therefore built with alternating straight and angled lines. The traverse was the name given to the angled parts of the trench.

5 = Barbed wire.
Barbed wire was used extensively in the trench warfare of world war one. It was laid, several rows deep, by both sides to protect the front line trench. Wire breaks were placed at intervals to allow men access to no man's land. However attackers had to locate the wire breaks and many men lost their lives through becoming entangled in the wire and shot.

6 = Listening post. (Sap)
Listening posts were used to monitor enemy tunnelling activity. They were usually approximately 30 metres in front of the front line trench and the listeners used stethoscopes placed against the walls.

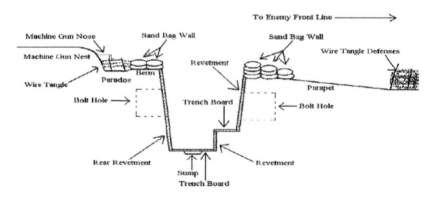

Wooden boarding was employed as a walkway and for walls to prevent collapsing. Sump holes were dug below the level of the lower trench boards to facilitate water drainage. Continued immersion in water led to a condition known as trench foot. The picture below speaks for itself the flesh is rotting on the bone.

A Severe Case of Trench Foot

A higher trench board was introduced as a fire step, this enabled soldiers to see and fire towards enemy positions.

Bolt holes were built into the front and rear walls, they were shored up with wood and corrugated iron and used for sleep, eating and protection, they were big enough to contain about three men.

LATRINES

What is not shown in this diagram is a latrine facility. It was usually a deeply dug hole, allowed to fill with water, with a planking system over for the men to squat on. This feature became a target for snipers, mortar and artillery and was a very smelly health hazard.

LICE

These nasty little creatures were a permanent part of life in the trenches. They laid eggs in the seams of clothing and soldiers would run the seams of their clothes along the flame of a candle to kill the eggs. They lived in the woodwork of the trenches and by the time men were relieved from trench duty and went for de-lousing their skin would be raw from continual scratching. The infestations were a major factor in sleep deprivation.

RATS

A serious problem and best described by the memoirs of Private Thomas McIndoe 12th Battalion of the Middlesex Regiment:

Rats! Oh crikey! If they were put in a harness they could have done a milk round, they were that big, yes, honest. Nearly every morning, a bloody great thing would come up and stand up on its back legs and gnaw at something. I used to line the sights up and give them one round of ball. Bang! And blow them to nothing.

This aerial photograph shows a trench system on the western front. It shows forward positions and communication trenches to support trenches. It is not known where this photograph was taken, but the layout looks similar to the Leipzig salient, two rows of trenches within the salient (North to South bottom of picture to top).

The duty relief system at this time was four days in the front line followed by four days in close support and then four days rest in billets about three quarters of a mile to the rear. When in the front line, whenever possible, the front line firing trenches were relieved every night. It was found that a longer period caused the instance of sickness to go up very rapidly. This last comment is taken from the war diary and it does not state whether the rotation was done by troops in the support position or merely that the front line troops relieved themselves with a stand to and stand down system. The diary mentions the details of life at rest.

"*When resting every effort is made to keep the men fit, and to rest them: Hot baths are supplied and if possible clean washing for every man, short route marches, fatigues work, classes of instruction etc are carried out. There have been no actual operations, the fighting being confined to intermittent shelling of our trenches, hardly a day passing without some shelling and artillery duels. As regards infantry there has been continued sniping, mostly by night and not so heavy by day, occasional more by nervousness that anything else*".

This last entry was made at the end of January 1915 before John arrived but it is relevant as the trench routine was the same and the facilities for rest the same. The bathing was often carried out at Field Ambulances and de-lousing carried out at the same time".

FIELD AMBULANCES

The Field ambulance was not a vehicle but the most forward of the Royal army medical corps (RAMC) units and the first line of documentation. There were three field ambulances attached to each of the 75 Infantry divisions. In action, two of these ambulances were in forward positions and the other was held in the rear. When the division was out of the line the field ambulances were allocated special tasks such as a scabies centre or for other ailments, a Divisional Rest Centre (DRS), or as a bath unit. If the latter, it was usually sited in a brewery where up to fifty men could be bathed at a time in the large vats and local women were used for laundering and the repair of clothing and uniforms.

Unusually John Banner's medical record is still available and the following entries are made:

31/7/1915 Boils. Admitted 9th Field Ambulance. ED/639 7/8/15.
27/8/1915 Admitted 7 Field Ambulance Quinsea.
4/11/1915 Rheumatism. Admitted 76 Field Ambulance. ED3459.
9/11/1915 To duty. ED/3695.
6/7/1916 Killed in Action.

GAS

The first recorded use of gas is by the French in August 1914 who used tear gas grenades containing xylyl bromide, a form of tear gas, in an attempt to stop the German advance through Belgium and north eastern France. The Germans first used it in October 1914 when they fired gas shells at the French positions at Neuve Chapelle. These shells were designed to cause violent sneezing thereby causing incapacitation rather than serious injury or death; both types were an irritant rather than a killing agent. Poison gases were developed by all sides once static trench warfare had commenced in an effort to create greater mobility. Poison gas in the form of Chlorine gas was first used by the Germans against the French in April 1915. The green cloud travelled towards the French lines and caused devastation and panic. The initial thoughts were that it was a smokescreen and all available resources were brought to the frontline in preparation for an attack.

British hood masks

1915 Tubular type gas mask, German 1915

By early 1916 all sides were using gas designed to kill or cause grievous injury. The dangers were not just immediately to the intended victims, wind change could cause the gas to be diverted back towards the users and gas residues remained in the bottom of craters and trenches for some time after deployment. Work in Saps was endangered by gas residues; on three occasions in April 1916 men became gas casualties whilst working underground.

TRAINING AND SPORT

During time at the rear further training was given in the use of hand grenades and time was also spent in drill and parades. The men were also encouraged at times such as these to get involved in sport; this helped with fitness and encouraged a healthy camaraderie.

Football was obviously a very popular sport, inter-company and platoon championships were held. This appears to have been encouraged across the BEF as post war football became a sport attended in 'unprecedented levels'. Cross country running was used for competitive and fitness training purposes. Boxing features occasionally in the diary and towards the end of March 1916 a two day competition was held in a barn. Fighters went on to represent the regiment in inter-regimental tournaments. Musketry competitions were held and those winners represented the regiment in divisional competitions.

More unusual sports included;

- Pillow fighting.
- Mess carts
- Relay obstacle
- Tug of war
- Inter-company ploughing. On 26th March 1916 with the use of horses borrowed from transport and three French ploughs, three older men who had been in farming prior to joining up held a ploughing competition, D company were the winners.

FOOD

A total of 3,240,948 tons of food was sent from Britain to the soldiers fighting in France and Belgium during the First World War and the British Army employed 300,000 field workers to cook and supply the food. At the beginning of the war British soldiers were given 10 ounces of meat and eight ounces of vegetables a day. As the size of the army grew and the German blockade became more effective, the army could not maintain these rations and by 1916 this had been cut to six ounces of meat a day. Later troops not in the front-line only received meat on nine out of every 30 days. The daily bread ration was also cut in April 1917. The British Army attempted to give the soldiers the 3,574 calories a day which dieticians said they needed, however, others argued that soldiers during wartime need much more than this.

Soldiers in the Western Front were very critical of the quantity and the quality of food they received. The bulk of their diet in the trenches was bully beef, bread and biscuits. By the winter of 1916 flour was in such short supply that bread was being made with dried ground turnips. The main food was now a pea-soup with a few lumps of horse meat. Kitchen staff became more and more dependent on local vegetables and also had to use weeds such as nettles in soups and stews. The battalion's kitchen staff had just two large vats, in which everything was prepared. As a result, everything the men ate tasted of something else. For example, soldiers often complained that their tea tasted of vegetables. Providing fresh food was also very difficult. It has been estimated that it took up to eight days before bread reached the front line and so it was invariably stale. So also were the biscuits and the soldiers attempted to solve this problem by breaking them up, adding potatoes, onions, sultanas or whatever was available and boiling the mixture up in a sandbag.

RELIGIOUS OBSERVANCE

During John's time with the battalion the Chaplain was Reverend L G Dickenson from Downton in Wiltshire. There are a number of references to church services and parades in the war diary although it was not a requirement to make such an entry. It seems that when there was nothing better to write about then the service got a mention. Some services were voluntary and some compulsory. The services were primarily Church of England but "non conformist services" were also held. Six other chaplains served with the battalion during the war and all these held Captains rank. The chaplain must have been an influential figure as in 1917 Lieutenant Wait mentioned the previous incumbent of the post in a letter home:

"We have sacked our padre and just got a new one. Our other was an awful man, full of gloom with a face as long as from here to Boulogne. He used to creep round the traverses on all fours grasping Woodbines. The men used to call him "Creeping Jesus". Very blasphemous I know, still very funny!! The new one seems a bit cheery & he has a parish near Maidenhead & he used to know Grandfather very well."

PART V

JUNE-DECEMBER 1915

A VISIT FROM THE BRASS

On 8th June 1915 the battalion was visited in the trenches at Hooge by the Divisional Commander, Major General Haldane. An account of the visit is given by his Aide de Camp who describes the General as; in a hurry. He also describes the trenches; as such a maze of works and debris that a day would be needed to realise where you are. It rained without warning and they were soon soaked, the trenches became a few inches deep in water almost immediately. Unusually this visit is not mentioned in the war diary

On Wednesday 9th June 1915 the Battalion returned to Ypres in the early morning and went into dugouts, built into the ramparts. They rested until 18th June when they returned to take up front line positions again at Hooge. During this rest period an accident occurred with a Lyddite grenade resulting in the death of an officer plus one other man and 23 others being wounded. This is a huge number for a grenade and presumable the reference is to a type of stick grenade which preceded the Mills Bomb. This weapon had a steel container, designed to create fragmentation injuries, which was filled with a solidified acid which on initiation caused a huge explosion. The numbers involved would suggest close proximity of men and perhaps a training session gone wrong, dropping this device could initiate the explosion.

JOHN'S FIRST OFFENSIVE ACTION; BELLEWARDE

On 16th June 1915 the trench routine was disrupted by an attack on the German lines.

1st Wiltshire   *Wednesday 16th June 1915.*   *Belgium, Menen Road*

2.50a.m. our artillery commenced bombardment on German trenches situated between ROULERS railway and Southern end of Ypres Wood.

4.20a.m. The 9th Bde had carried the first line of German trenches and 1 platoon of C Coy assaulted trench at S end of Ypres Wood which was taken without difficulty. A bombing party started to work up the enemy's trench in the direction of HOOGE and made rapid progress. The remainder of C Coy & D Coy followed up. The leading men (5a.m.) reached a point some 100yds from HOOGE village; meanwhile a Communication Trench was dug from culvert under Menen Road to S end of Ypres Wood and endeavours made to join up two pieces of German trench running E towards HOOGE. Until 6a.m. the situation remained unchanged.

6a.m. More progress towards HOOGE was made – a point within 50yds of the village being reached in the German trench. Between 6a.m. and 9a.m. the situation remained unchanged. Work of barricading and reversing the parapets was continued.

9a.m. The Germans advanced down two CTs from the N and under cover of a heavy fire started bombing heavily. We replied with grenades, this exchange lasted about 1 and a half hours.

10.30a.m. Our supply of grenades became exhausted and the Germans succeeded in driving us slowly back down the trench. In retiring we suffered heavy casualties during the period of the action.

11a.m. We evacuated the eastern portion of the German trench. We retired in the open and lost a considerable number of men in doing so. A counter charge was organised about this time to check the enemy's advance, but without success, as the officer and many men were shot down and the remainder made no progress.

3p.m. Germans commenced a heavy bombardment of Ypres Wood and the trenches which had been captured in the morning. Our guns replied by shelling the German's about BELLEWARDE Lake, presumably to break up any attempt at counter attack. The situation remained unchanged in our trenches.

6.30p.m. Germans started a very heavy bombardment of Ypres Wood which lasted about 1 hour.

8p.m. Germans fired a considerable number of gas shells in the neighbourhood of the Menen Road but these only caused temporary inconvenience.

11p.m. Suffolk's started digging trench parallel to C trench from corner of Ypres Wood to culvert. The trench running eastwards from the corner of Ypres Wood was abandoned and blocked over a distance of 30yds.

The casualty toll for this action was nine officers and nearly 200 other ranks killed, wounded or missing. The day's work was part of a larger action against the Bellewarde Ridge. This ridge was well placed for enemy observation and represented a bulge into the allied lines, the long term objective being to straighten the line and gain the high ground. Careful preparations had been made for the attack with triple communication lines being installed, and patrols mounted by the Royal Flying Corps (RFC). The men were equipped with extra ammunition, grenades and wire cutters. It appears the attack failed as successive lines of assaulting troops got mixed up and confused, this caused the attack to lose its impetus. The attack was continued on 22nd June, following a half hour bombardment by artillery, which left the German positions intact, two platoons of A company attacked the German positions but were stopped by effective machinegun fire. The attack failed this day, a dismal failure.

WEAPONS USED

.303 calibre Lee Enfield Short Magazine Bolt Action Rifle (SMLE)

The .303 Lee Enfield rifle, introduced in 1895, was the main military service rifle of the British Empire and her Commonwealth countries for over 60 years. Over this period of time it went through various upgrades and modifications, the model shown had a five round magazine. It was a single shot, bolt action design and was still Britain's service rifle in 1939. It was not declared obsolete and officially replaced until 1941 with another Lee Enfield, the No 4 rifle. Both models stayed in use until the end of World War Two. The cost of production of each rifle was £3 15s (£3.75p). This rifle was faster to recycle rounds than the German Mauser of the day as the firing pin was cocked on closing the breech as opposed to being cocked on opening the breech. A proficient user of this rifle could fire 20 to 30 aimed rounds per minute, often German troops reported encountering machine gun fire when in fact they had been repelled by well-trained rife men armed with the Lee Enfield SMLE rifle, often called Smelly.

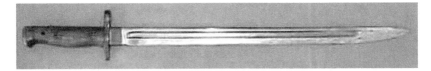

Bayonet

The standard issue bayonet for the SMLE rifle was about half a metre long (blade 43cms)

Mark One Mills Bomb

In 1915, a grenade developed by William Mills, a Birmingham engineer, began to be used by British troops. The bomb had a central spring-loaded firing-pin and spring-loaded lever locked by a pin. Originally it had a seven second fuse which required that the bomber held the bomb for three seconds after ignition otherwise the enemy could throw it back before it exploded. In later models once the Mills Bomb was in the air, the lever flew up and released the striker, which ignited a four-second time fuse, allowing the thrower to take cover before it exploded. When the grenade exploded the cast-iron casing shattered producing a shower of metal fragments. The grenade developed by Mills soon became very popular with British soldiers and remained in short supply until the end of 1916. By the time the Armistice was signed, more than 33 million Mills Bombs had been issued to soldiers in the British Army. Prior to the introduction of the Mills Bomb a stick type grenade was in general use.

For the next six months the battalion continued its pattern of static trench warfare in the Hooge area. The diary records a daily routine of shelling, fatigues, religious services, repairing trenches, wiring and of course a regular tally of those killed and wounded. It seems that not many days went by without casualties from one cause or another, usually shelling or snipers.

NOTABLE EVENTS DURING THIS PERIOD WERE:

- An attack on German trenches on 22nd June. The attack was preceded by a 30 minute artillery bombardment starting at 7.30 p.m. and at 8 p.m. the men went over the top. The attack was beaten back by machine gun fire resulting in one officer killed, two officers and 24 other ranks wounded, the artillery fire had caused little damage.
- 23rd July command of the Battalion was taken over by Lieutenant Colonel Brown.

On 26th August the Corp Commander visited the men in the trenches in the company of General Haldane.

- At this time the companies of the Wiltshire Regiment were taking turns in occupying a mine crater, part of the line near to Hooge. The day following the visit by senior officers B Company were in occupation and A Company were given orders to occupy and reinforce a nearby old advanced trench which linked with the adjoining regiment the 2nd South Lancashires. A bombing party accompanied those digging and a grenade throwing fight ensued with the enemy. During this engagement 500 grenades were thrown at the advanced German trench resulting in one man killed and seven wounded. The Company were relieved at 2.30 a.m. and rejoined the Battalion who were then relieved in turn and withdrew to bivouacs North West of Dickebusche.
- Throughout 1st and 2nd September the trenches occupied by John and his comrades were subjected to intense artillery bombardment resulting in 18 men killed 64 men wounded and a further two men missing believed killed. This action

caused General Haldane to send the following message, *"Convey to Wiltshire Regt my appreciation of stout hearted manner they stood bombardment yesterday. Regret heavy casualties"*.

- On 14th October movement orders were received and the Battalion moved to a camp at Busseboom, the 7th Brigade of which the Wiltshire Regiment was a part of were being transferred from 3rd Division to 25 Division's 2nd Corp. This movement was part of the planning for the divisions being raised by Kitchener and it was necessary to place experienced and professional units with these newly raised units to provide operational experience. On 17th October the Battalion was inspected by General Haldane who made a speech to bid them farewell from 3rd Division. The Battalion responded with a three cheers and set off on their way to the sound of 'Auld Lang Syne' played by the 3rd Division band.

The rest of October, November and December 1915 were spent in the trenches at Ploegsteert Wood, Belgium, out of the line at rest in Papot France or the Piggeries, Belgium. There is much mention in the diary of route marches, bomb throwing training and sniping. The Wiltshire snipers seem to have been very successful claiming many German lives.

CHRISTMAS 1915

The newspaper report of John's death dated 29th July 1916 reported various facts concerning his life and service, one of which that he had been at home on leave for Christmas 1915. It is not known for how long or where he spent the leave but whilst John enjoyed the comforts of home and Christmas festivities his comrades at the front were back to the trenches.

Although the War Diary entry for Christmas 1914 makes no mention of the unofficial truce, or any form of fraternisation which had been experienced along the Western Front that year, there was no repetition in 1915 as strict orders against fraternisation had been issued to the whole British Expeditionary Force (BEF). Friendly overtones were made by the Germans but these were ignored by the 1st Wiltshires.

1st Wiltshire Friday   24th December 1915   Belgium, The Piggeries.

Battn went into trenches and relieved 8 LN Lancs. The parapet had suffered considerably through rain.

Casualties Two in the evening: L/Cpl Tugwell was wounded in the head by rifle bullet and Pte Morgan was wounded while on a listening post. Weather fine after a rainy dawn.

1st Wiltshire Saturday 25th December 1915 Belgium, Ploegsteert Wood

Weather very mild. Enemy was quiet all day: A white flag which was shown above their parapet was fired on and withdrawn: and opposite the left company a German shouted out a question as to the attitude we intended to adopt, but no reply was given. The repair and drainage of trenches was carried out as usual. The Corps Commander visited the Battn Boxing Day was equally quiet and the men engaged in trench repairs. The diary notes the death of L/Cpl Tugwell who was wounded on the 24th.

PART VI

1916

NEW YEAR

New Year's Eve was spent in reserve; half the battalion got a bath and the other half got fatigues!

1st Wiltshire   Saturday 1st January 1916   France, Papot

This day was kept as a holiday by the Battn. Only one fatigue party was required in the morning and there were no parades. The men were given a dinner of pork, Christmas pudding and beer, and at 5p.m. a pierrot party consisting of six officers and one man, entertained a crowded house at the ROMARIN recreation room. At 8p.m. all officers dined together.

A Pierrot party was fancy dress and no doubt the seven entertainers put on a cabaret show dressed in whatever they could make up from materials at hand.

At this time a daily rum ration was allowed. The memoir of Corporal Charles Quinell of the 9th battalion, Royal Fusiliers tells the story:

"The one thing we used to look forward to every night was our issue of rum. That was very, very acceptable. It used to come

up with the rations in a 2-gallon stone jar, and that was given to the company sergeant-major – there were four platoons in the company – and the platoon sergeant would come along the trench of a night-time with a big table spoon and this mess tin full of rum. The cry was 'Open up' and you'd open your mouth up and he'd pour this tablespoon full of rum down your throat."

On 3rd January the battalion returned to trenches at Ploegsteert Wood and relieved the 8th Loyal North Lancashire Regiment who returned on 7th January. John and his comrades experienced action during this stay in the form of artillery duels, mortar and hand grenade exchanges. Casualties were light but the snipers accounted for eight Germans.

LEWIS GUN SECTION FORMED

The diary tells us that on 7th January 1916 a Lewis gun section was formed. Prior to this each Battalion had its own machine gun crews armed with the Vickers Maxim water cooled heavy machine gun. This weapon had a crew of between six and eight men, but supplies of the weapon were slow in coming to the front as the Vickers Company could not make them in sufficient numbers, they even allowed American companies to make them under licence. At best Vickers produced 200 guns per week. On 14th October 1915 the Machine Gun Corps was formed and all guns and crews transferred to this specialist formation. Training and parades for the Lewis gun section is mentioned a number of times but it wasn't until 17th April that the section first saw action.

1st Wiltshire   Monday 17th April 1916   France, La Targett

Mine fatigues. During the night there was a considerable amount of bombing after the explosion of an enemy mine, it was thought that the enemy had got into part of the outpost line and blocks were put up, but it was subsequently discovered that the trench was clear. The Lewis rifle of A Coy was brought up from the support line and did effective work.

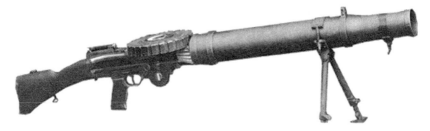

Lewis Light Machine Gun

The Lewis was a light machine gun, developed in the United States in 1911. At 12 kg it was far lighter than the Vickers Machine-Gun and in 1915 the British Army decided to purchase the gun for use on the Western Front.

Another advantage of the Lewis is that six of these guns could be made in the time taken to produce one Vickers gun. Although too heavy for efficient portable use, it became the standard support weapon for the British infantry during the First World War. It used either a 47 or a 97 round cylindrical magazine and fired the .303 calibre rifle round used in the Lee Enfield Rifle.

IN RESERVE

On 8th January 170 men attended the divisional training school at Nieppe, in total 1500 men attended this event but no one from the chemical division turned up to do the gassing. The men returned for fatigues on trench repair. On 9th January the same party returned and received their training, it is reported that there were no casualties and the new tubular masks worked very well.

From 12th January to 9th March John and his comrades moved to Outterstene France where they spent time in reserve, training, route marches, sports and alerts were created to keep the men fit and active.

On 25th February the 2nd army chemical adviser supervised a demonstration of the German flammenwerfer (flamethrower). The purpose of this demonstration was stated as to show the men how harmless the weapon really was! This weapon was feared by infantrymen as its purpose was for clearing trenches by burning to death all those therein, the demonstration was no doubt done as a morale booster. The weapon consisted of two tanks one with a high pressure gas such as nitrogen and the other with petrol and a thickener. The fuel was propelled down a tube by the gas and ejected from a lance which had an igniter in the end. The flamethrower was often operated by two men one who carried the bottles in a backpack and the other operating the lance, these units were closely followed by riflemen whose job it was to hold any trench cleared by the flames. The first use of the Death's Head symbol, made notorious during the Second World War by some SS units, was by the flamethrower operators.

RETURN TO THE FRONT

On 10th March 1916 the battalion left Outterstene and commenced a route march south to move into the area controlled by 17th Corps. The first night was spent at Robecq and the second day's march ended at Valhoun where they then spent five days. The area had been evacuated the day before by the French as the BEF had agreed to take responsibility for a further 20 miles of front. The diary for the second day makes some interesting remarks.

1st Wiltshire   Saturday 11th March 1916   France, Robecq

The Battn proceeded upon the second stage of the march at 8.15a.m. the destination being VALHUON S of PERNES. After passing through LILLERS the country became more interesting and hills and slag heaps rose into view. VALHUON was not reached until 2.45p.m.: in spite of the length of this second march very few men fell out. The village had only been evacuated by the French a few days before and in consequence the billeting of the first English troops proved a matter of not little difficulty. However, by the next morning the billets had been made habitable. About 10p.m. a draft of 42 other ranks arrived from St POL: of the 42 no less than 36 were men who had either been wounded or sick.. Some had been with the 5th Battn in the Dardanelles, some were from the 2nd and the remainder had been previously serving with the 1st. The physique showed a great improvement on that of previous drafts and the men were younger but only 6 had seen no active service.

Even with rests this is a second gruelling physical day, for the diarist to mention the few drop outs gives an indication of the high level of fitness, discipline and morale of the men at this stage.

By this stage in the war replacements were usually fresh faced recruits straight from home with no experience. To receive battle experienced replacements, 36 out of 42 must have been exceptional to warrant a note in the diary. On 16th March the journey south continued to Ternas where they occupied more French billets, the march south was about 80 miles in total.

The battalion remained in situation until 11th April 1916 during which time it continued various training and route marches.

1st Wiltshire   *Tuesday 11th April 1916*   *France, Savy*

The Battn relieved the 11th Lancs Fusiliers in the support line NE of LA TARGETTE. It was preceded in the morning by an advance party consisting of the first relief of the working parties. There were no casualties in the course of the relief. The work taken over consisted mainly of carrying for both French and English mining companies in the front line and this work continued day and night by means of a series of reliefs, which were each of about eight hours duration.

MINES

Mining was a tactic now employed by both sides and consisted of sinking a shaft or sap in the forward face of a home trench to about 25 feet, (dependent on the geological conditions prevailing) and then tunnelling towards the enemy trenches. At a point directly underneath the objective a chamber would be constructed and packed with explosives. The mine would then be detonated, usually at the commencement of an attack and troops sent forward to capture the crater left by the explosion.

The objective of the mine differed, some were placed directly underneath the enemy trench or position with the purpose of killing as many soldiers as possible and others were placed strategically to create a crater forward of existing positions. In both cases the purpose was to gain territory and immediately on initiation of the mine, attacking troops would move forward to consolidate the position. Defending troops would attempt to stop the position being held thereby denying the enemy an advantageous position.

During the course of tunnelling soldiers were in constant danger from tunnel collapse, naturally occurring gasses, attack underground and poison gas. The poison gasses used by all sides were designed heavier than air to enter trenches and it tended to drop to the lowest point. There are instances of tunnel walls collapsing due to the proximity of an enemy trench going in the other direction, a fire fight would then break out underground.

Miners in a tunnel   Destruction of a trench

Tactics to prevent the enemy taking advantage of a successful mine were practised in training. This involved the immediate deployment of men armed with small arms and grenades to the crater to defend against attacking troops. 1ˢᵗ Battalion seemed to be good at this tactic and the potential advantage of a mine could be turned against its instigator as described in the following diary entry.

1st Wiltshire   *Thursday 4th May 1916*   *France, La Targette*

During the day enemy was very quiet. Work was carried on in the trenches connecting the new craters and the outpost line and at four posts steel loophole plates were inserted. At 7.55p.m. an enemy mine was sprung just to the S of the already existing crater at the top of Grange CT: a post of two men was buried and 2nd Lieut Clark, D Coy, who was also buried was extracted after five hours work. He suffered only from bruises and shock. The effect of the explosion was to fill in the already existing crater and form a large plateau, the near edge of which was consolidated. By this mine the enemy put himself in a worse position than formerly in the way of sniping. 2nd Lieut Sainsbury, D Coy, again did good work. The casualties were:-

Missing believed killed Ptes Hursey and Dudman of C Coy. Wounded Pte Ellis.

The battalion stayed in the line until 1ˢᵗ June 1916, this period was the longest they had ever spent in forward positions, 21 days. The diary shows a picture of constant work and fighting with a steady flow of casualties. There were numerous mines detonated by both sides. On 9ᵗʰ May the battalion was visited by Brigadier General Heathcote and shown around the trenches. At 7.46 p.m. the Germans 'welcomed him with another mine'. The diary goes on to say that the event was not unexpected and the area was evacuated prior to the detonation. I suspect that this must have been led by precise intelligence as imprecise information would not have allowed the evacuation at the right time and place and for such a distinguished visitor to be present and in potential danger. This would indicate intelligence from a prisoner as opposed to a listening post which would give location of tunnelling activity but not target area and initiation time. Following this explosion, the 1st Wiltshires were soon on the lip consolidating the position and some heavy bombing ensued. This last probably refers to hand grenade bombing between attackers and defenders as by this stage hand grenades, called bombs at the time, were in widespread use both as an attack and defensive weapon.

RETURN TO THE REAR

On 1st June the Battalion, having been relieved in the night by the 5th Seaforths, undertook a two day march to billets in the divisional training area at Chelers. They were joined on this day by 40 replacement other ranks posted for duty with the Battalion from the 2nd Hampshire Regiment. The record for the next two weeks shows the Battalion training in open warfare for six hours every day except Sundays. This training was designed to familiarise the men with working as a unit within a grand design. It started with Company practise in deployed formations, bayonet fighting and advancement in artillery. The next stage was training as a Battalion with the cooperation of Lewis Guns and bombers, the whole Brigade then practised the capture of enemy second lines after the first line had been taken and the assault of targets beyond that point. During this period the Battalion received one Lieutenant, nine Second Lieutenants and 233 other ranks (including the 40 of the 2nd June) as reinforcements. The Battalions strength was now recorded as; 42officers and 939 other ranks.

On 14th June the Battalion commenced a two day march south to a location at Barly, northwest of Doullens arriving at 3 p.m. Two men dropped out of the march on the second day but rejoined the Battalion that evening when the award of two Distinguished Conduct Medals, a Military Cross and a Military Medal were announced.

On 16th June 49 other ranks men arrived and the fighting strength is now noted at 986 other ranks. This made the battalion at full strength and the day was spent with Company kit and weapons inspections. The following day the Companies practised bayonet fighting and the erection of bivouacs. After dark the

Battalion marched to Gezaincourt arriving at their billets at 1.30 a.m..

The rest of June was spent training particular bayonet practice for all ranks including officers. The development of initiative and leadership was encouraged and fire control was practised with an emphasis on the junior NCO ranks. four more night marches were made with a final destination at Varenness, during this time three more Second Lieutenants joined the Battalion.

The last entry made by Lieutenant Colonel Brown for June 1916 concluded with: "*On the night of 30th June/1st July the Battn marched to VARENNESS in the forward area of impending operations*".

PART VII

BATTLE OF THE SOMME

INTENTION

The battle of the Somme was originally conceived and planned to be the main allied push on the western front for 1916. The location was determined by enemy action which commenced in February 1916 in the Verdun area, a major offensive against the French by the Germans. During this offensive, which was designed as a battle of attrition, the French had suffered huge losses and pressed the British to mount an offensive to relieve pressure on them by diverting German resources north of Verdun. The French commander for this battle was Marshal Petain, who became a national hero known as the Hero of Verdun. Following the fall of France in World War Two Pétain formed a collaborative government and was subsequently convicted by a post war tribunal and sentenced to life in prison where he died aged 95.

There were three main objectives for this battle, as described, by then, General Douglas Haig to:

1. Relieve the pressure on Verdun.
2. Assist our Allies in the other theatres of war by stopping any further transfer of German troops from the Western front.
3. Wear down the strength of the forces opposed to us.

PREPARATION FOR THE ATTACK

The battle took place along a 25 mile long front in the area of the Somme River commencing on 1st July. The attack was preceded by a weeklong artillery bombardment where 1,738,000 shells were fired. The bombardment was originally scheduled for five days with the attack commencing on 29th June, but the attack was postponed for two days due to bad weather and the bombardment itself extended to seven days.

The artillery bombardment was interspersed with pauses to trick the defending Germans to man the front line trenches in anticipation of an attack, and used combinations of high explosive and shrapnel shells for differing purposes. The intentions of the artillery action were to:

- Cut the defensive barbed wire, disrupt and destroy the enemy trenches leaving them no protection from the attacking infantry.
- Kill as many enemy soldiers as possible and leave those that survived disorientated to the point of being incapable of defence.

The main perceived threat was from counter attacking enemy troops, held in support or reserve positions, against the troops occupying the captured German front line trenches. With that in mind, the first waves of attacking troops in addition to their personal arms and kit, carried picks and shovels to repair the trenches damaged by the artillery bombardment. It was clearly expected that the artillery bombardment would create a situation of no resistance to the advancing first wave of infantry, who would then take possession of the trenches and repair them in preparation to defending the captured positions.

GERMAN PREPARATIONS

In advance of this offensive the Germans had strengthened their defences in the region. It had been blatantly obvious, due to the massive build-up of armies and resources in the area of the Somme, that an offensive was imminent. No great effort was made to keep allied intentions a secret. Three successive lines of defences followed the high ground across gently undulating farmland. Thickets of barbed wire were placed in front of the lines. Machine guns in concrete strong points were deployed with interlocking zones of fire, most sited to fire into the flanks of attacking infantry. The chalky soil was ideal for tunnelling and German engineers burrowed deep to create almost indestructible shelters for the troops in the front line. German artillery was placed further to the rear, well camouflaged from the air, but ideally situated to deluge no man's land with high explosive and of course their own lines when overrun by allied troops. Artillery spotters were well placed to direct fire with telephone communications, the cables of which were buried deep enough to survive artillery bombardment.

THE OFFENSIVE BEGINS

On 1st July seventeen mines placed under German front line positions were detonated and at 7.30 a.m. officers blew their whistles and tens of thousands of men climbed the ladders out of their front line trenches and advanced at a steady walk towards the enemy front lines. The steady walk was designed to ensure that lines remained intact and did not become disorganised.

The cessation of the artillery bombardment was the signal for the German defenders to leave the sanctuary of their deep bunkers and man the defences. The bombardment had failed on at least two counts, it failed in many places to cut the barbed wire and also to destroy defenders and defences. The advancing troops were met by a hail of murderous fire from the German Maxim machine guns and the artillery counter bombardment. On this first day the BEF sustained 57,470 casualties, of which 19,240 were killed or later died of their wounds.

The sight that greeted the dawning of 2nd July is described by George Coppard, a machine gunner at the Battle of the Somme:

"The next morning (July 2nd) we gunners surveyed the dreadful scene in front of us......it became clear that the Germans

always had a commanding view of No Man's Land. The British attack had been brutally repulsed. Hundreds of dead were strung out like wreckage washed up to a high water-mark. Quite as many died on the enemy wire as on the ground, like fish caught in the net. They hung there in grotesque postures. Some looked as if they were praying; they had died on their knees and the wire had prevented their fall. Machine gun fire had done its terrible work."

This was the scene along 25 miles of front.

JOHN BANNERS LAST DAYS

John Banner's last few days of life are best described by the accurate reproduction of the battalion's war diary. I have tried to pinpoint a specific location and time for his death but there are a number of confusing factors that mean that assumption can be wildly inaccurate. For instance, for the date records show he was killed, the action commenced at 7 p.m. of the evening before. At this specific time all four companies of his battalion were committed to the common purpose of defending the trench captured from the Germans a few days earlier. The action continued until relieved the day after his death and then not until nightfall. The war diary would have been written up after relief and is a little confusing and devoid of fact. What is known is that John died whilst defending a captured German trench in the Leipzig Salient on 6th June 1916. At the time of his death the trench was subjected to a heavy artillery bombardment. His name has been carved on the Thiepval memorial which means that he does not have a known grave and either his body was obliterated or damaged to a condition beyond recognition. Whilst the diary previously mentions individual deaths, during this engagement the casualties were too high to record everyone by name. The other factor relevant to this non recognition is that bodies were lying unrecovered for long periods of time. Enemy snipers and artillery spotters targeted any recovery attempt making such action impossible. Natural decomposition could have made John's body unrecognisable or expedient to bury into mass graves when recovery did become possible. The one factor which would have pinpointed with greater accuracy where and how John met his death was which company he belonged to. A local Bromsgrove newspaper reported John's death and the brief circumstances; the source of this information, a letter to the family from John's Company Commander has unfortunately not survived. The section of the diary for 5th July (into the early hours of the 6th) where I believe John was killed along with the Commanding officer, Lieutenant Colonel Brown, is shown in bold print. This is the only section of the diary which fits all the known clues and places him in the first captured German trench shown on the map as A.

The official history states that the enemy troops in the Leipzig Salient at this time were the Guards Fusiliers

The diary tells the rest of John's story:

1st Wiltshire   Saturday 1st July 1916   France Varennes.

9a.m. The day was spent resting after the previous nights march, preparations being made for the coming offensive.

1st Wiltshire   Sunday 2nd July 1916   France Varennes

A full kit inspection of all companies in battle order was made by the CO. Church Parade by Rev L Dickenson was held at 11.30a.m. Battn at 1 hours notice. At 3.15p.m. orders were received to proceed to HEDEAUVILLE. The Battn moved off at 4.10p.m. and marched to bivouacs outside the village. At 7p.m. orders were received for Battn to proceed to bivouacs in AVELUY Wood via BOUZINCOURT. At this juncture the B team (those officers, NCOs, and men not taking part in the first assault) left the Battn and joined the Divisional Train at VADENCOURT. A team spent the night in the Assembly Trenches in the wood.

1st Wiltshire   Monday 3rd July 1916   France Aveluy Wood.

The day was spent resting. One stray shell caused 2 casualties in the Battn (16 in all of the other regiments). At 9p.m. the Battn moved via Black Horse Bridge to the fire line. D & C Coys to our

old front line trenches. A Coy to Leipzig Salient 300 yards of trench previously captured from the Germans (on July 1st). B Coy were in support in Tobermory St and sent up 2 platoon to the help of A Coy. Battn HQ at Campbell post just off Campbell Ave CT. Enemy shelled heavily at midnight for about one and a half hours. Battn relieved in this position 1st Dorsetshire Regt. Highland Light Infantry Manchesters.

Black Horse Shelters beside the River Ancre, 150 yards south of Authuille and 1½ miles south of Thiepval, in which the 15th H.L.I. spent rest periods before the Battle of the Somme. 1916.

Black Horse Bridge

1st Wiltshire   Tuesday 4th July 1916.   France Leipzig Salient.

Trenches in front of Leipzig Salient. Battn line was D Coy extending to Thiepval Ave and relieving the 11th Cheshire Regt & 8th Borders. A Coy continued to consolidate the Leipzig Salient and extended their line to the right by 150yards erecting barricades. About 12.30a.m. a heavy hostile attack was directed against our position in the Leipzig Salient, the enemy were seen to leave their trenches and from information from a prisoner captured it was found that they attacked in waves of 2 platoons. At 12.30a.m.

a very intense bombardment on our front line and continued till 2a.m of 5th.

  Casualties:- wounded 11 Killed 1.

Soldiers of the Wiltshire regiment attacking on the Somme

1st Wiltshire   Wednesday 5th July 1916   France Leipzig Salient

Enemy continued shelling. Shortly after mid-day orders were received that the whole Battn was to move into the old enemy trench in the Leipzig Salient with a view to an attack on the enemy 2nd line, which was very strongly held forming the Leipzig Redoubt. The length of line to be attacked was about 600 yards and necessary operation orders were issued. At 4p.m. however the length of objective was changed to 300 yards. Operation orders were issued as follows. C & D Coys were selected to do the assault, C Coy on right and D Coy on our left. B Coy half to form carrying parties, half in support. The attack was carried out in following order Attacking wave of each company, C & D, 3 platoons In support 1 platoon Two platoons of B Coy were carrying parties, one to each attacking Coy. The remaining half Coy of B were in support holding the line of the Quarry. The time originally appointed for the attack was 6p.m., this was afterwards changed to 7p.m. For half min before this, there was an intense artillery bombardment assisted by Stokes Mortars, punctually at 7p.m. our

1st wave advanced to the attack under heavy rifle and machine gun fire. D Coy on the left under Capt R L Knubley reached their objective without heavy casualties, but D Coy on the left were badly cut up by machine gunfire and though they reached their objective were insufficient in numbers to withstand the heavy German Counter attack which followed immediately, and were compelled to withdraw temporarily. The second wave of each Coy consisting of 1 platoon had followed on the first wave at an interval of about 30-40 yards. C Coy on the right were followed by the carrying party of 1 platoon of B Coy. After the trench had been cleared of Germans, all dugouts were bombed immediately and then took in hand the consolidation of the position gained. Barricades were erected in all the communication trenches leading to the German 3rd line and bombing parties posted. In the case of 1 CT the Germans had erected a strong barricade prior to the attack. Two blocks were also built on the left of the captured trench, the second about thirty yards behind the first as a precautionary measure in case retirement became necessary. The men in this attack were magnificent, all showing the greatest coolness and initiative. Officer casualties in this attack were: –

D Coy 2nd Lieut Starkey, missing. Lieut Holman, wounded (later died of wounds). C Coy Lieut G W Penruddocke. 2nd Lieut Troughton.Very shortly after the attack commenced the enemy began an intense bombardment chiefly directed on their old front line now occupied by our HQ and support company, especially on that portion of it into which the Russian Sap entered, an underground tunnel from the old British front line excavated before first offensive of July 1st 1916.In this bombardment 1 shell made a direct hit on the trench killing Lieut Colonel W S Brown and wounding RSM Parker and 2nd Lieut Stockbridge the Battn Signalling Officer. Capt A H Hales acting 2nd in Command who was directing the attack from the line of the Quarries having also been killed, Capt R L Knubley took Command of the Battn until the arrival of Capt S S Ogilvie from the B team. Other officers brought up from the B team were 2nd Lieut Sharpe, 2nd Lieut J R Tayler. Prisoners taken during this attack 41.Approx Casualties Killed 20. Missing 22. Wounded 158. Missing believed killed 2.

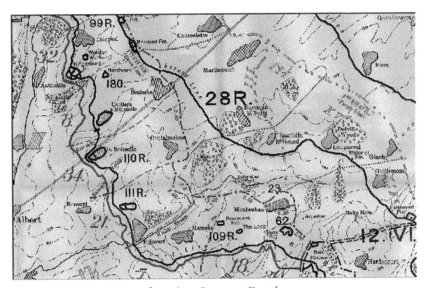

Map showing Somme Battle area.
The Leipzig Salient is shown just to the right and below
the red number 32

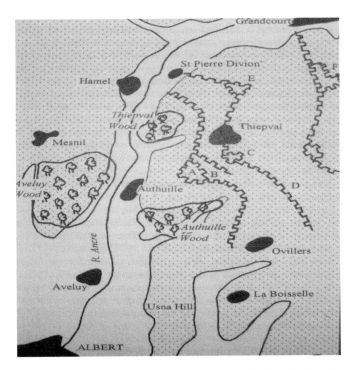

A = Leipzig Salient   B = Hindenburg Trench
C = Wonder Work   D = Hohenzollern Trench
E = Schwaben Redoubt   F = Stuff Redoubt

1st Wiltshire   Thursday 6th July 1916   France Leipzig Salient

(morning) On the extreme right of the captured trench communication was now opened via an old CT with a Company who were
holding the line behind. C & D Coys were relieved about 5a.m.
and went back to Tobermory Street reaching there at 7.30a.m.
Two Coys of the 3rd Worcestershire Regt took their place in the
captured trench and carried on the work of consolidation. In this
attack the casualties were roughly as follows:-
  Killed Colonel W S Brown and Capt A H Hales
  Missing 2nd Lieut Starkey
  Wounded Lieut Holman, 2nd Lieut Stockbridge, 2nd Lieut
J R Tayler
  Lieut Penruddocke and 2nd Lieut Troughton.
    Throughout the day the enemy carried on with intermittent
bombing, trench mortars and rifle grenades. Shelling was
continuous the whole day, but was not of the same intensive
nature as during the attack. In the evening C & D Coys were
again brought up into the Leipzig Salient, C Coy taking over from
the line they had capture on the night of 5th July. A Coy were
placed in the Quarries to relieve the other Coy of 3rd Worcs Regt.,
D Coy taking the place of A Coy in support. The 2nd Coy of the
3rd Worcs Regt relieved and returned to reserve in the 2nd line of
old British trenches.

1st Wiltshire   Friday 7th July 1916   France Leipzig salient

12.15a.m. On the early morning of the 7th orders were received
that another attack would be made on the same objective as that
attacked by D Coy on night of 5th. This was known to be the very
strongest part of the Leipzig Redoubt. While the conference about
this attack was being held, a very violent hostile counter attack
was made on the trench captured by C Coy. This commenced
about 1.15a.m. The enemy attempted to rush the trench from the
front and both flanks, also working down the C T trenches with
the first sudden rush they managed to reach the very edges of the
trench into which they dropped bombs and opened fire. Lieut R J

A Palmer the only officer in the trench and the men under him with great coolness beat off this attack and inflicted heavy casualties on the enemy. Very heavy bombing followed in the next 2 hours and intermittently until 5.30a.m. D Coy in this attack were pushed up to the support of C Coy from Battn HQ. The attack on the left was timed to begin at 9.30a.m. and orders for the operation were as follows:- A & B Coys under Lieut Gosden OC A Coy, were selected to make the assault. The attack was made in 2 waves each consisting of 3 platoons, the remaining 2 platoon held in reserve. At 9.30a.m. After 30secs intense bombardment by guns and Stokes mortars, the assault was made and the trench successfully captured. This was not accomplished without difficulty as the enemy did not seem to be taken by surprise, manning their parapet very heavily as our troops arrived. Previous to the assault our snipers had been placed in the shell holes in front of their line and fired 30 rounds of steel nosed bullets at the machine guns which had caused so many casualties in the previous attack by D Coy. Whether silenced by our snipers or by the bombardment, at any rate the enemy machine gun did not fire during our advance. During this advance Lieut Gosden was killed, 2nd Lieut Ross wounded and 2nd Lieut Sharpe wounded and missing believe killed. This left 2nd Lieut Clegg Commanding the trench. 2nd Lieut Snelgar being in charge of carrying parties in Quarries.1p.m. In this attack a large number of Germans were killed and 23 were taken prisoner, 5 of them being wounded. The captured trench was consolidated but being very wide afforded very little cover. But for incessant bombing from the left flank, no great difficulties were experienced until about 1.30p.m. when the enemy opened a terrific bombardment with high explosive. There was practically no protection in any part of our position particularly in the newly captured trench and in the Quarries. The bombardment lasted for about 5 hours and our casualties were enormous about 160. Two Coys of the 3rd Worcs Regt who had been utilised as carrying parties were now put in to reinforce the line and suffered equally heavily. 2nd Lieut Clegg and 2nd Lieut Snelgar were both wounded and Capt Knubley was sent up to direct operations. 2nd Lieut Hayward C Coy was also wounded slightly in the hand but *remained at his post and was afterwards killed. Other casualties were Lieut L A H B Morris, killed, 2nd Lieut Petter wounded, 2nd Lieut S J Terry (Adj) wounded. Capt R L Knubley wounded, died of wounds later. Casualties among NCOs and men about 219. At about 6.30p.m. 2 Coys of the 3rd Worcs Regt and 2 Coys of the 8th Loyal North Lancs Regt under the Command of Lieut Col Davidge 3rd Worcs. The Battn went into dugouts at Crucifix Corner.*

The casualties killed and wounded over the few days of this engagement are recorded as 26 officers and 400 other ranks. The fighting strength of the battalion is also recorded as 200 men. (There is a numerical anomaly here as the battalions fighting strength was recorded as 986 on 16th June).

The accuracy of the diary is questionable as the Commonwealth War Graves Commission site shows the actual casualties over the period 5th – 7th July as 79, the majority of these casualties are shown on the Thiepval memorial. The best guess of the experts interpreting the diary at The Wardrobe is that John was recorded as one of 22 missing after the action of 5th July along with 20 killed in action and 158 wounded. One other possibility is that he could have been one of two casualties reported *'missing believed killed'*. The defended trench was subjected to an artillery bombardment and these two men could have been killed by an exploding shell and no mortal remains left behind. The anomaly of date of death is most likely that the action where he became a casualty was commenced on the 5th and continued through the night into the 6th.

PART VIII

AFTERMATH AND
CONCLUSIONS

If John's body was recovered and buried in an unknown grave, he could lie in any one of over 200 cemeteries dedicated to the horrendous loss of the Battle of the Somme. Lieutenant Colonel Brown, John's Battalion Commander, who was killed in the same artillery bombardment as the one which I believe killed John, was buried in a nearby cemetery named 'Blighty Valley Cemetery, Authuille Wood'. This cemetery contains 1027 graves; all but three being British, with 536 of those graves containing unknown soldiers. This cemetery is located very near to the Leipzig Salient and is largely used for the casualties of early July 1916; perhaps John's mortal remains lie in rest there. There is also the possibility that Johns body was never recovered and lies in the ground where he was killed. Almost every year remains of soldiers are recovered from these fields and with the science of DNA some re identified and laid to rest in a marked grave.

John was the Banner family's only casualty although they provided three combatants. The family grieved their loss and his picture was placed in an appropriate frame as shown in the cover picture. The local community eventually commissioned a memorial at All Saints Church which honours the 36 local men lost in this terrible conflict. By the year 2006 John Banner was almost forgotten, with one elderly family member knowing of his existence but not having known him. The interest in compiling a family tree recovered this situation and now John's memory is treasured by his descendants.

Norton War Memorial, All Saints Church
Birmingham Road, Bromsgrove

The 1st Wiltshire Regiment remained in France, as a fighting unit, until the end of the war and then demobilisation commenced almost immediately. The last group of officers and men totalling 65 embarked for England on 29th May 1919.

1st Wiltshire   Monday 11th November 1918   France, Berlaimont

11.00. Instructions received that HOSTILITIES were to cease at 11.00 and that defensive measures to be taken and that no intercourse was to be held with the enemy.

Lieut Col G B Ward, DSO returned from leave and assumed command of the Battn.

12.45. Battn proceed by March Route to BEAUFORT. Battn HQ established at W.14.d.2.7. Sheet 51.

Appx
SPECIAL ORDER OF THE DAY BY
GENERAL HON. SIR J H G BYNG, KCB, KCMG, MVO.
Commanding Third Army
11.11.18
To all Ranks of the Third Army
The operations of the last three months have forced the enemy to sue for armistice as a prelude to peace.

Your share in the consummation of this achievement is one that fills me with pride and admiration.

Since August 21st you have won eighteen decisive battles, you have driven the enemy back over sixty miles of country and you have captured 67,000 prisoners and 800 guns.

That is your record gained by your ceaseless enterprise, your indomitable courage and your loyal support to your leaders.

Eleven Divisions in the four Corps (Guards, 2nd, 3rd, and 62nd, 5th, 37th, 42nd, and New Zealand, 17th, 21st, and 38th) have been continuously in action since the beginning of the advance and have borne the brunt of the operations. Other Divisions have joined and left, each one adding fresh lustre to its history.

To all ranks, to all Corps and formations, to all administrative and transport units, I tended my thanks. May your pride in your achievements be as great as mine is in the recollection of having commanded the Army in which you served.

J BYNG, General, Commanding Third Army.

The Battle of the Somme is commonly remembered for its atrocious losses on the first day. However historical research is now showing that this battle was a training ground for the allied armies to develop training, practices and tactics which led to the victory of 1918. The failures and successes experienced by the BEF in 1915 led to a system of self-analysis which continued during and after the Somme. The Somme demonstrated that standards of training, particularly in rifle fire and methods in attack, varied greatly throughout the army. Successful tactics developed by one unit were previously, not necessarily spread throughout the BEF. In trying to turn a large number of civilians into soldiers quickly, the army found it necessary to standardise its procedures. From the summer of 1916 onwards, a series of training pamphlets were produced. They summarised the lessons learned on the Somme, laid down simple instructions for combat operations, and made sure that British soldiers adapted to the new demands of the modern battlefield. The war diary gives an insight into this concept when it describes training; leadership to the next level was encouraged.

One of the objectives of the Somme battle was to make the Germans suffer great losses, a war of attrition. British losses were 420,000; French losses were 200,000 and the Germans 500,000. The Germans did suffer grievous losses, but as to whether or not the battle was a failure on this point is dependent on how many men each side started with and how many losses they could absorb and continue the fight. The fact that Germany eventually sued for a cessation of hostilities would indicate they were losing the war of attrition. It must be remembered, however, that America entered the conflict in 1917 providing a fresh source of meat for the grinder. The battle certainly relieved pressure on the French forces around Verdun and tied German forces to the Somme area. As for territorial advantage, the furthest forward the front moved was seven miles but it did cause the Germans to retire to the defensive positions of the Hindenburg Line.

The week long artillery bombardment failed due to a number of factors. The Germans were well prepared and defended against the assault. By 1916 the original B.E.F. professional army was all but gone, as were a lot of the original volunteers. Conscription had commenced and a large proportion of the men of the munitions industry had gone to the army to be replaced by women and older men. This factor created a lack of experience within the manufacture of shells and a large proportion were failing to explode. A large proportion of shells fired were of the shrapnel type ideal against personnel but not of much use for the intention of cutting the barbed wire and destroying defensive positions.

The area of the conflict where John died, Thiepval, proved too heavily defended to be taken by direct assault and only fell later when the area was outflanked and attacked during September 1916. The battle continued until 18th November 1916.

In the course of the battle, 51 Victoria Crosses were won by British soldiers. 31 were won by NCO's and 20 by officers. Of these 51 medals, 17 were awarded posthumously 10 to NCO's and seven to officers.

Did John Banner give his life in vain? I have my opinion and I hope I have given sufficient information to provoke an opinion. I do believe that the evidence shows John Banner was a brave and adventurous man who had a sense of duty and served his country with honour.

1. He followed the call to join at a time when there was no obligation other than moral.
2. He took a path away from that which was encouraged to find new experiences and friends.
3. His service record, such as exists, shows a dutiful man with a minimal sickness record, all three entries are serious provable complaints, no bad backs! None of the sickness coincides with any event of note in the war diary.
4. Young men join armed services for various reasons, during peace time for career, adventure, escape, service and during war time for all the same reasons but also to defend home and family. In my estimation John Banner joined up for all of these reasons and paid the ultimate price, but Britain's way of life was preserved and his family all lived long and fruitful lives.

John Banner surely fits my definition of hero!

JOHN BANNER'S MEDALS

The 1914 -1915 Star

Authorised in 1918, to award those who saw service in a theatre of World War One, between 5th August 1914 and the 31st of December 1915. Those eligible for the 1914 star were not entitled to the 1914-15 star.

Personnel entitled to a 1914 or 1914-15 Star would automatically qualify for the War Medal 1914 – 1920 and the Victory Medal 1914 -1919.

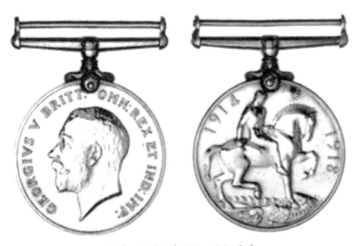

The British War Medal

This medal was approved in 1919, for issue to officers and men of British and Imperial forces who had rendered service between 5th August 1914 and 11th November 1918. The medal was automatically awarded in the event of death on active service.

The Victory Medal

This medal was issued to all those who received the 1914 Star or 1914-15 Star, and to most of those who were awarded the British War Medal, it was never awarded singularly.

ABOUT THE AUTHOR

Mick is a retired British police officer having served in both Birmingham City and West Midlands forces. He served in both uniform, CID and other specialist units gaining experience and expertise in major investigation. In retirement he has combined two lifelong passions, motorcycling and history, resulting in research trips throughout Western Europe and books about the two world wars.